Essential Workers, Like Me!

Written By
John D. Skalbeck and Samuel T. Skalbeck

Illustrated By
Kadeja Liggins, Ameara Wahhab, Erin Bagatta,
Hana Shiozaki, Leland Starwalt, Silvia Bond, and
Tessa Weber

Skalbeck Books

Written By
John D. Skalbeck and Samuel T. Skalbeck

With contributions from
Sridevi Gopalakrishna Reddy

Illustrated By
Kadeja Liggins, Ameara Wahhab, Erin Bagatta,
Hana Shiozaki, Leland Starwalt, Silvia Bond, and Tessa
Weber

Graphic Design and Layout By
Hana Shiozaki

Proceeds from this book go to Reading is Fundamental
www.rif.org

Skalbeck Books, LLC
Copyright © by John D. Skalbeck 2020

Fill in a name that starts with an N

N______ likes nurturing newborns.

N______ could be a nurse like me!

C_______ likes collecting crops.

C_______ could be a farmer like me!

T_______ likes tidying up toys.

T________ could be a custodian like me!

G_______ likes
going to grandma's.

G________ could be a caretaker like me!

F_______ likes finding facts.

F________ could be a scientist like me!

B______ likes
baking brownies.

B_______ could be a cook like me!

L_______ likes
leading lessons.

L________ could be a
teacher like me!

Fill in a name that starts with a D

D_______ likes going door to door.

D_______ could be a delivery driver like

F________ likes fiddling with fires.

F________ could be a firefighter like me!

C_______ likes counting coins.

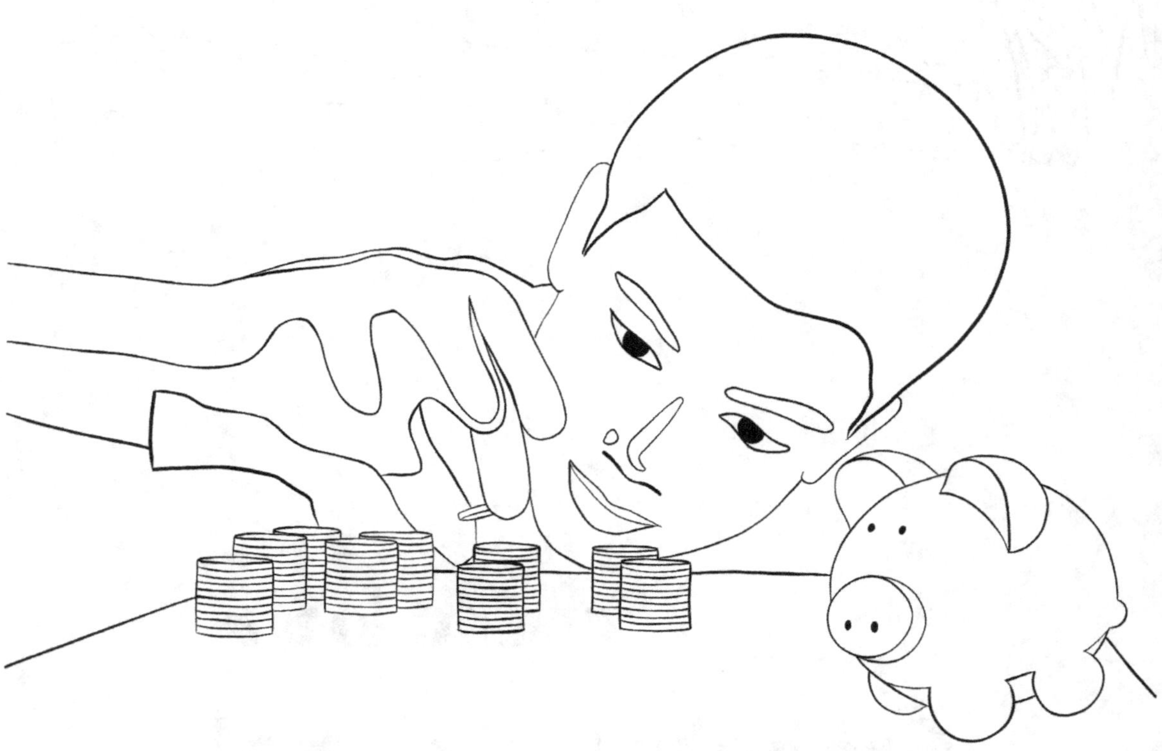

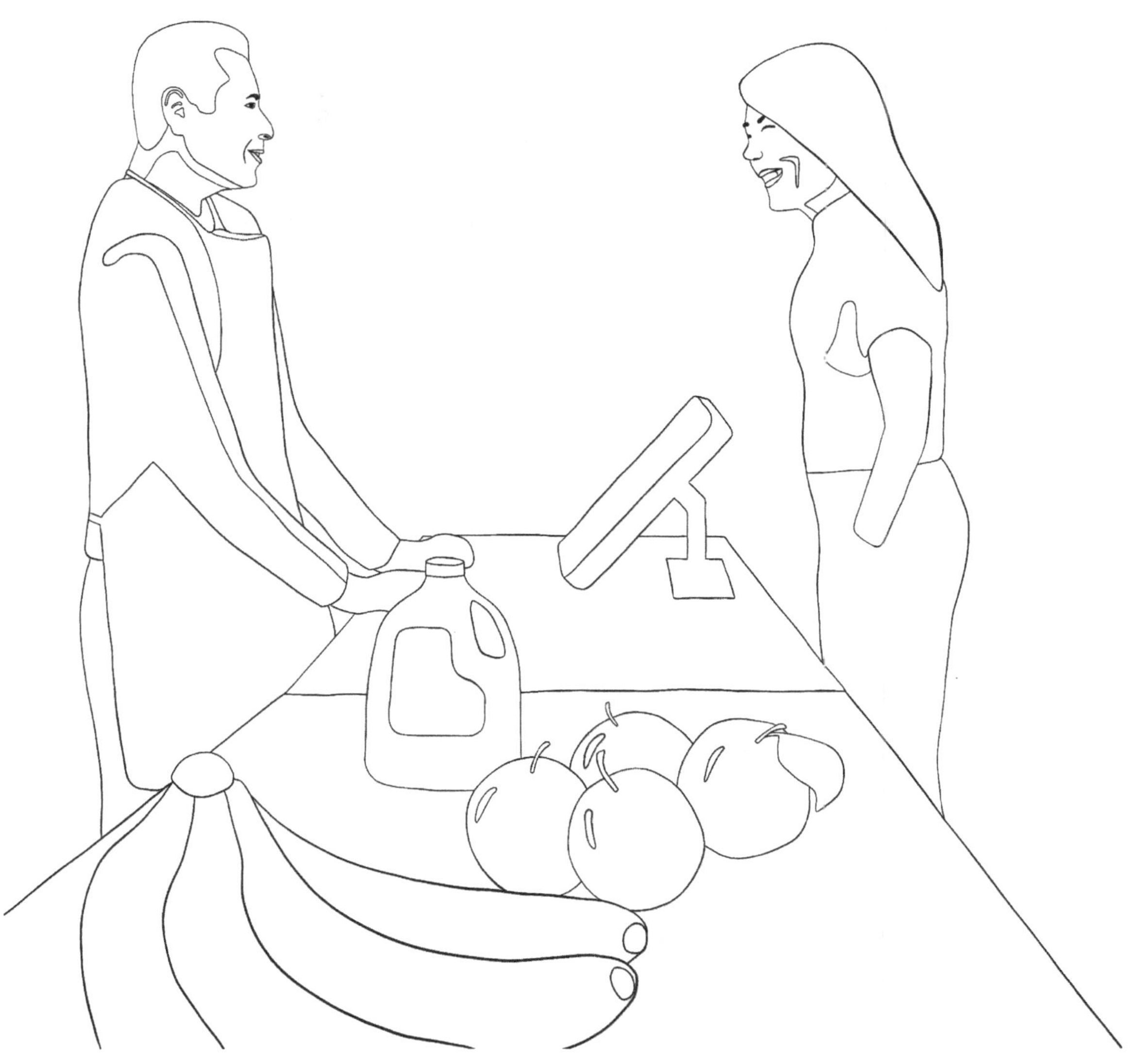

C______ could be a cashier like me!

P_______ likes protecting people.

**P________ could be a
soldier like me!**

C______ likes

caring for creatures.

C________ could be a doctor like me!

STOP
SAFETY PATROL
Pursue
your passion.

Be yourself
like me!
STOP
SAFETY
PATROL
2+2=4

THANK YOU

Essential Workers, Like Me! was made possible by the creative donations of the Illustrators. Learn more about these talented artists from their websites listed below.

ILLUSTRATORS

Cleo and Frankie by Ameara Wahhab
@amearawahhab, www.amearawahhab.com

Bailey and Pat by Tessa Weber
@tessacweber, www.tessaweber.carbonmade.com

Greta and Casey by Erin Bagatta
@erinbagatta, erinbagatta.com

Tao and Dakota by Hana Shiozaki
@shio._.hana, www.shiohana.com

Finn by Kadeja Liggins
@kligg.co, www.kligg.co-square.site

Carson by Leland Starwalt
@lelandstarwaltdesigns

Nyomi and Lucy by Silvia Bond
@daly.doodles

PROCEEDS FROM THIS BOOK GO TO

Reading is Fundamental, the nations largest literacy non-profit that engages communities to ensure all children have the ability to read and succeed.

www.rif.org

DONATIONS

Contributors for this book encourage readers to also consider donations to the following worthy causes:

Communities in Schools of Richmond
https://www.cisofrichmond.org/

United Way
https://www.unitedway.org/get-involved/ways-to-give/donate

Black Lives Matter
https://blacklivesmatter.com/

United Nations Relief and Works Agency
https://www.unrwausa.org/

Mental Health America
https://www.mhanational.org/

Shanthi Bhavan Children's Project
https://www.shantibhavanchildren.org/

LitterRally
https://www.litterrally.com/